Ghost
HOUSE

a novel

by

PAUL KROPP

🗗 Dominie Press, Inc.

CHAPTER 1

It started with me shooting off my mouth. The four of us were walking down Barton Street on the way to school. I was with my little brother, Zach, like always. A.J. and Hammy were going down the street with us, A.J. riding on his bike and Hammy with his skateboard.

We were goofing around, like always, when we passed the old Blackwood place. It's a big old house that used to belong to this lumber guy, back when our town was full of lumber mills and the river was chock full of logs. I guess the house must have been pretty nice back then. These days it's all boarded up, with half the roof sagging and the paint all peeled away.

"It's haunted, you know," A.J. said. His real name is Alexander, but we've called him A.J. ever since we were little kids.

"Riii-ight," I replied. "And I'm King Tut come back to life."

"No, I'm not kidding," A.J. went on. "My dad says that a kid got stabbed in there years ago. And I've been by here at night, and you can still see funny lights moving around inside." He sounded all pumped up, like he was actually scared.

"Must be some high school kids having a party," Zach told him, "trying to find some place to crash where the rats won't get 'em."

Hammy zoomed up the sidewalk to the steps on his skateboard, and then did a 180 Ollie that looked pretty slick. "Hey, ghosts!" he shouted. "How do you like that? You want to see me do a grind?"

"See?" I told A.J. "The ghosts didn't say a thing. They didn't even give Hammy a round of applause. If that place is haunted, how come the ghosts are so quiet?"

"It's quiet as a tomb," my brother threw in. He

made his voice real deep for the "tomb" part, sort of like *tooom*!

"You guys shouldn't joke," A.J. came back. "There's more to this world than you and me understand."

"Like ghosts?" I asked. "How about witches and warlocks and frogs that turn into princes?"

"But only if they're kissed, right?" my brother added. Then the three of us all broke into big laughs.

Laughing is what the four of us do best. We'd been laughing together ever since... well, ever since ever. We were together in preschool, friends in grade two, and best buddies since grade six. Except my brother, of course. He's not my friend, because he's my brother, and also because he's a dork sometimes. But still, the four of us are always hanging together. If ever there is a ball game, we become half the team. If there is a movie to see, we all go together. If there is a problem, then all of us have to fix it. Like the time Hammy's line drive smashed Mrs. Headly's window. We all chipped in on that one. After all, it was my baseball, A.J.'s bat, and Zach's pitch that got the ball going. We're that tight.

But that doesn't mean we always agree on stuff. Hammy, for instance, takes school very seriously. He studies all the time, which is funny for a skater. A.J. is really the jock in our group. He follows all the sports there are, even golf, and he plays half of them pretty well. My brother, well, he's just a junior version of yours truly. Except that about a year ago he got to be the same size as me. People think we're twins. Teachers at school call us Double Trouble: "Here come the McCann brothers. Better watch out."

Not that we're bad, really. We're just a little bit "smart mouth" sometimes.

"You guys should listen up," A.J. said. He was getting that serious voice, like we were about to make some big mistake. "Somebody got killed in that house, way back when. My dad told me about it. People say it's been haunted ever since. That's why no one will buy it. The place has a curse on it."

"Whooooo! Whooooo!" my brother said, and then began laughing.

"Yeah, right, I'm really scared," I laughed.

"You guys make me so mad," A.J. told us. "Halloween's coming up, and there's no telling what might happen. Stuff isn't as simple as you think."

I shook my head and looked hard at him. "A.J., there are no ghosts, anyplace. There's just no such thing. When you're dead, you're dead," I said. They were the same words my dad used to say.

"Unless you're a mummy!" my brother shouted, and then he began walking with his arms stretched out, mummy style. We'd done that for a play last year for the little kids in grade two. They thought it was great.

A.J. got a funny look on his face, and then smiled at the two of us. "Okay, if you guys are so brave, I've got a deal for you. Spend one night in the Blackwood house—one full night—and I'll, um." His voice trailed off.

"You'll what?" I asked, challenging him.

"I'll give you fifty bucks," he announced.

"Fifty bucks to spend a night with cobwebs and rats?" I replied. "You've got to be kidding! How cheap do you think we are? We could make almost that much baby-sitting."

"Okay, how much?" he asked.

I turned to my brother, Zach. We both knew that A.J. was the guy with money. He was the one whose family had the big-screen TV at home and the fancy Lexus in the garage. A.J. gets more money for allowance than my sister gets working the cash register at the supermarket.

"A hundred bucks each," Zach said. He drives a hard bargain. I think he'll go into business some day and make millions.

The money made A.J. stop and think. Two hundred bucks is a lot of money. For a kid in grade eight, like me, it's a *ton* of money. We knew that A.J. had the cash. I once saw his savings account passbook, and he had a good five thousand just sitting in the bank. But would he take the bet?

"Deal," A.J. replied. He turned to Hammy so he'd listen up and then laid down the terms. "A hundred each. You've both got to stay inside for twelve hours, like five in the evening to five the next morning. No leaving. No sending out for pizza. You come out even once, and you lose. And if you lose,

then you've got to give me that baseball you've got,
the one autographed by Mark McGwire."

"No way," we both shouted.

"That's a World Series ball," I said, though A.J.
knew it full well. "Our dad got that for us. I mean,
you've got to be dreaming to think we'd ever give
that to you."

"Okay, so you loan it to me, for a month."

"Just a month. And no touching it too much," I
said.

"What, are you backing out? You think you might lose the bet? I thought you guys had some guts."

I looked over at Zach. We were both thinking the same thing.

"We're not backing out," I replied. "We're in. Hammy is the witness. Two hundred bucks versus the Mark McGwire ball."

"Deal," A.J. replied.

"Deal!" I said, holding out my hand to shake his. "Kiss the money good-bye, A.J."

CHAPTER 2

"It's dark in here," Zach said when we made it inside the old Blackwood house.

"What did you expect?" I asked him. "You think the ghosts are going to pay the power bills and turn on the lights? I mean, once you're dead, it's really hard to earn money."

"Very funny, Tyler," he told me. Then he turned back to the plywood-covered window that we had crawled through. "You're not going to hammer those nails back in, are you?" he shouted to A.J.

"No, I'm using duct tape. You break the tape before I come back, and you lose the bet. Twelve hours, Zach. No sneaking out halfway through."

"Yeah, yeah. A deal is a deal," my brother sighed.

It hadn't been that easy to get inside the old Blackwood house. All the first-floor windows were covered with sheets of plywood. We found one piece that people couldn't see from the street, and then used a crowbar to pull it free at the bottom. With A.J. holding it out, there was just enough room for Zach and me to crawl inside.

"I'll be back at five in the morning. If you haven't chickened out by then, I'll help you get out," A.J. said, his voice muffled by the plywood.

"And if the ghosts get us first, you'll see that we get buried real nice, okay?" I shouted.

"No problem," A.J. laughed. "You want a nice coffin, like walnut or cherry, or will one of the cheap cardboard ones be okay?"

"I'll be dead, so it won't matter to me," I laughed. "Tell my mom to save the money and buy herself a decent car."

"It's your funeral!" A.J. called out, and that was the last we heard from him. The only sounds outside were the wind blowing and a few trees scraping against the house.

I turned on the flashlight and cast the beam around the room. There wasn't much to see. Somebody must have sold off all the couches and chairs a long time ago. All that was left were a few small cupboards, a couple of bookcases built into the wall, and an old mattress on the floor. The house was cold, of course, and it looked as if the pipes had all burst. There were brown stains on the walls and big pieces of plaster hanging down from the ceiling.

"Really deluxe," I said to Zach.

I flashed the beam of light into the kitchen, catching a small shape moving along the floor. *Mice*, I said to myself. *Or rats*. Then I shivered a little. That mattress could be full of them.

Between this room and the next one, which might have been a dining room, there was a big central staircase. Unlike the rest of the house, the staircase seemed to be in pretty good shape. I was about to ask Zach if he wanted to go explore, when I heard the music.

"Hey, you hear that?" I asked him. "It sounds like music. Can you hear it?"

Zach was silent, and that seemed a little weird. "Can you hear it?" I repeated, louder than before.

Still nothing.

"Zach!" I shouted, turning the flashlight beam right onto my brother.

The kid blinked back at me. Zach had on a pair of headphones and was busy bopping his head to some music.

"You idiot!" I snapped, pushing one headphone off his ear.

"Hey, don't break them," he snapped. "It's the only fun thing I've got for tonight. Unless you want to tell ghost stories."

All I could do was shake my head. Not only was my brother pretty fearless, he still had a wicked sense of humor.

"Look, I think we might be better off upstairs," I told him. "Those windows aren't all covered over, so there'll be some light. Besides, I think there are mice down here, or maybe rats."

"You afraid of mice?" he asked.

"Yeah, I'm afraid of mice. Want to make something of it?" I shot back.

"No problem, Tyler. I was just checking. I kind of hate mice, too. Remember those stories we used to get in first grade, all about those cute little mice. I kept wondering, who thinks mice are cute? Gotta be sick, if you ask me."

"Okay, let's go," I told him.

The two of us grabbed our backpacks and moved toward the stairs. The floor creaked, of course, but at least it didn't give way under our weight. Still, we had to be careful. The whole house shook like it could collapse in a strong wind. And there was no telling how bad the wood had rotted over the years.

The stairs, just as I'd thought, looked to be in pretty good shape. We got about halfway up before one of the steps cracked under my weight. After that, I was a little more careful. I wasn't afraid of ghosts, but falling down a bunch of stairs is no fun. I've done it myself and had the broken bones to show for it.

We were almost at the top of the stairs when

something slammed down below. I jumped, and I could feel Zach do the same.

"You hear that?" I asked him.

"Yeah," he said. "A door or something. The way the wind just blows through the house, it probably blew a closet door closed."

"Yeah, probably," I agreed.

Still, the two of us took the last few steps a little faster.

When we reached the second floor, there was enough light coming in from outside to see down the hall. The Blackwood house must have been a pretty nice place a long time ago. There were four doors coming off each side of the hall, probably with a bedroom behind each one. Down at the end was an arched window that showed a big oak tree outside.

CRRR-AACK!

Lightning. Zach and I froze, counting the seconds. *KA-BOOM!*

"Great," Zach told me. "We've got mice downstairs, a storm outside, and I bet a leaky roof over our heads. This is going to be one fine night."

"Keep your eye on the prize," I told him. "Two hundred bucks. Ten twenties, twenty tens, forty fives."

"Eight hundred quarters," my brother continued, "four thousand nickels."

"Hey, your math is pretty good," I told him.

"But a nickel doesn't buy much," he replied. "Actually, a hundred bucks won't buy all that much, either. It's just that I really love taking money from A.J. That kid is so rich, he deserves to give some away. And besides, there's no way I want his hands touching the Mark McGwire ball. That would be too…"

"Degrading," I finished for him.

"Pretty good vocabulary," he said. Zach took the headphones from around his neck and put them back on his head. Then he reached down to his waist and pushed a button on his MP3 player.

Then Zach swore.

"Hey, watch your mouth," I told him. He may be as big as me, but that doesn't mean I can't tell my little brother what to do.

"This thing's dead," Zach whined. "I just put

fresh batteries in, and now, nothing. You must have busted the thing when you pushed the headphones."

"Riii-ight," I told him. "Like I could kill your batteries by pushing on the headphones. Really good science, Zach."

"Okay, Mr. Science," my brother said. "How come your flashlight is starting to blink on and off? How come it's getting so dark in here?"

CHAPTER 3

I'm pretty good at science. It's the one thing I like about school, and our science teacher is pretty cool. Last year I came up with a wicked science fair project. I used our basement to grow all sorts of pea plants. I proved, in case you ever wondered, that toothpaste and ground-up cheeseburgers do *not* help plants grow.

But right now I was at a loss. The batteries in Zach's MP3 player were good for up to eight hours. Okay, so they don't really last for eight hours, but he should get four hours from them, at least. And my flashlight had three brand-new C cells. I mean, those batteries had plenty of power.

The flashlight should have been good for most of the night.

But there was a big storm going on outside, and I knew that did strange things. There's stuff like ball lightning that we can't explain. The air can carry an electric charge that does weird stuff. Maybe if I were in college, I could tell Zach why our batteries were going dead. But I'm still just a kid, so I couldn't explain all that. There was nothing to do but find a place to flop.

"Pick a door," I told him.

"How come?"

"Because that's our room for the night. In this hotel, you get to choose the room you like because they're all empty."

"Pretty snazzy," Zach replied. "What if I pick the wrong door? Didn't we read some story about that? Something about picking the door with the tiger."

"Yeah, and there was a moral to the story— don't pick the door with the tiger. So pick," I told him, "before the flashlight goes out."

Zach picked the second door on the right. I knew he would. The thing about living with a guy all your life is that you know what he's going to do, mostly.

"Hey," Zach said, "the doorknob is cold, just like in the horror movies."

"The whole house is cold," I told him. "Just turn it and let's find someplace where we can sleep."

The knob creaked when he turned it, just like in a horror movie. But there was no ghost in the bedroom. We found no monster, no ghoul, no undead soul. There was only a broken chair, an iron bed with springs but no mattress, and a little sink.

"I hope you find this to your liking, sir," I told Zach. I tried to pretend I was a bellboy at a hotel.

"It looks just, uh, wonderful. Very clean," Zach said, nodding his head and slipping into the role of the gracious hotel guest. "I guess there's no need to worry about mice in *this* mattress."

"Indeed, sir, the Blackwood Hotel offers nothing but the best. I hope you enjoy your stay, sir. Remember that the hotel pool closes at ten o'clock."

Zach giggled. He always liked the stories that I used to make up. Back when he was little, when Mom or Dad didn't read us a bedtime story, I'd just make one up. Zach and I were always in the story, mostly as the heroes. The great thing was that I could just change the story as it went along. If Zach said, "Hey, I don't want to be the mummy," I could make him the son of the pharaoh, just like that.

The flashlight was so dim, it looked like I'd be telling stories all night.

KA-BOOM!

More thunder. The room flashed with light from outside, and then shook as the thunder boomed. Over in one corner, I could hear water dripping. The roof was leaking and rain was seeping down through the attic, through our ceiling, down to the floor, and then down to the dining room below. No wonder all the plaster was falling down.

Zach got out his sleeping bag, and I unrolled mine. Neither one of us wanted to try the bedsprings. We found two dry areas on floor and tried to get ready for the night.

Zach complained that his music was gone. I complained that I didn't have enough light to read a comic book. But once we settled into our sleeping bags, it wasn't all that bad.

I don't believe in ghosts, you see. I don't believe in all that spooky stuff. To me, that's just what they use to make movies. Like our dad used to say, "If you can't see it or touch it, it just ain't there."

Our dad is dead now. He's been gone for five years, ever since the accident, but I've never seen his ghost, or any ghost, for that matter. I mean, I'd like to talk to my dad if he could come back. There's a lot of stuff he didn't have time to tell me before he died. But there's no way dead people can talk to us. "When you're dead, you're dead," my dad used to say. And then he was dead himself, before any of us were ready for it.

I don't know why I was thinking about my dad, lying there on the floor in a sleeping bag. Maybe I felt a little guilty about fooling our mom. We had told her we were doing a sleepover at A.J.'s house, and she believed us. She always believes us. So I always feel bad when we don't tell her the truth. But there was no way she'd let us spend a night in the Blackwood house. Not for two hundred dollars. Not even for two *million* dollars!

"Tyler?" my brother whispered to me. "What are

you thinking about?"

"Nothing," I said. The last thing we needed was to start talking about dad and how we missed him.

"You think there might be mice up here, on the floor?"

"Nah, mice hang out where there's something to eat. There's no food around here, unless you have a really tasty big toe."

"I was just wondering," the kid went on.

"Because I heard something, and I thought it was mice."

I started listening when he said that. Outside, there was wind blowing at the house and through the trees. There must have been a branch or two beating against the house. I could hear a kind of pound, pound, pound. It was like the house was being hit with a brush. And there was one other sound.

"It's not mice," I said.

It was footsteps. Not even the usual footsteps, but very soft steps that I could just barely hear. It was more the floor creaking than the sound of footsteps, but there was something moving in the house down below us.

"There's something down there," I barely whispered.

Chapter 4

My brother swore again, not loud, but the words were there, hanging in the cold air.

"Shhh!" I told him. "You want to send out a news flash that we're up here?"

I got up on one elbow and listened hard. Again, there was so much noise from the storm that it was hard to hear anything in the house. There were sounds down below, but was it really footsteps? It could be a branch brushing against a wall, or a cupboard door blowing in the wind.

There was a flash outside and then more thunder, close enough to make the whole house shake.

I could hear Zach jump up, tense and ready.

"How come this flashlight won't work when we need it?" he whispered.

"We've been through that," I told him.

"So, what do we do now?" he asked.

There are times when Zach really acts like a kid brother. Like he thinks I'm that much smarter because I'm a year older. Truth is, I'm not all that smart, and I didn't know who or what we were up against. But I knew there was somebody in the house, somebody who was no friend of ours.

"It must be some homeless guy," I thought out loud. "He's probably more scared of us than we are of him."

"Yeah, probably," Zach agreed, but he didn't sound very convinced.

"So, it's no big deal, because it's a big house, right? Lots of rooms in this hotel, right?"

"Right," my brother agreed.

"So, get some sleep. There's no problem until there's a problem, right?" My dad used to say something like that. He was full of funny old sayings.

KA-BOOM!

More thunder. Not too much chance that either of us was going to get any sleep like this. A storm outside, water dripping from the ceiling, and some guy walking around downstairs.

Then there was a new sound. It was like metal, a sound almost with a ring to it.

"What's that?" Zach whispered.

"Don't know," I whispered back. It sounded like something metal being dragged along the floor.

"You ever see *Slingblade*?" my brother asked.

"Would you just shut up," I shot back.

My brain started working real fast. We had some guy downstairs, in the dark, dragging something metal. It was clanging now, like a chain. In fact, the more I listened, the more certain I became that it *was* a chain. Now, why would a homeless guy be carrying a chain?

Maybe the homeless guy wouldn't be too happy with the two of us flopping in "his" house. Maybe he carried a chain to get rid of kids like us. Maybe he'd start swinging the chain at our heads if he found us up here.

Real stupid, I thought to myself. We should have

brought the crowbar with us. That would have given us a weapon. As it was, all we had was the flashlight. If somehow I could hit the guy on the head with the flashlight…

I couldn't finish the thought.

"Tyler! The guy is coming up the stairs!"

Now it was my turn to swear. We could both hear the footsteps coming up the staircase, and the chain being dragged up each step and riser.

"He's coming for us, Tyler. The guy knows where we are!"

"Not if you shut your dumb mouth he doesn't," I whispered. "Get over to that side of the door. I'm getting on the other side."

"And then what?" Zach asked, his voice all high and scared.

"If the door opens, I'm going to hit him. I'm going to bring the flashlight down on his skull. And then we run like anything."

Zach did what I told him. If the door opened, it would get pushed right in front of him. The guy wouldn't see Zach, even if he made it inside.

Of course, if the guy looked to the right, he'd

see me right away. But if he kept his eyes straight ahead and stepped inside, I'd have one good shot at him. So long as I didn't miss, we'd get out okay.

The guy stopped at the top of the stairs, just down the hall. I could hear the chain rattling. When the wind died down, I could even hear him breathing. At one point, I thought I heard a little laugh.

Then there was a loud crack. The guy must have whapped the chain against the first door. There was a slam as the door smashed open. The guy's steps went into the bedroom right next to us. We could hear him pacing around, back and forth in the room, dragging the chain.

"Heh-heh-heh!" a voice cried out, a kind of muffled laugh. Then, suddenly, there was a smash against the wall.

CRAA-ANG! The chain hit against something metal, and I could feel the wall shake from the impact.

"Tyler," my brother whispered, "let's get out of here."

"Too late," I said.

The guy had already left the room next to us and was back out in the hall. He smashed open a door across the hall, and then came to a stop in front of ours. He was right outside our door, breathing heavily.

"Heh-heh-heh!" laughed the voice.

CHAPTER 5

Our door crashed open. We were both frozen, waiting, in the silence that followed. I could hear the guy's breathing. Even louder, I could hear my own.

One step and the guy was inside. It was so dark that it was hard to see him. I had the flashlight up high, ready to smash down on him, but I knew I only had one shot.

Then there was a loud grunt and the door went flying, right at the guy. Zach must have pushed it as hard as he could.

"Aw-ugh!" the guy screamed as the door smashed into him. There was a loud clump as he fell, and then the clank of the chain as it hit the floor.

"Let's get out of here," Zach cried.

"Yeah!" I agreed.

I yanked open the door and got ready to run past the dark shape lying on the floor. In two seconds, both Zach and I could be down the stairs. In ten seconds, we'd be out the window and running to the street.

I was halfway down the hall when I heard Zach shout out, "Hey, wait up!"

The guy on the floor was groaning, but he wouldn't stay down there forever. "C'mon!" I shouted. "Let's go!"

"Nah, we're not going anyplace!" Zach said. Then he moved over to the guy and put his foot right on his chest. "Come back here and check out your homeless guy."

I thought he was crazy, but what choice did I have? Slowly I went back down the hall, and then passed the dim flashlight to my brother.

"You ever see those running shoes before?" my brother asked.

I looked down at two big running shoes, a pair of high-cuts with a fancy design that glowed in the dark. I made the connection even before Zach beamed the flashlight at the guy's face.

"Hammy!" I said. "What the…"

"Get your foot off me," Hammy shrieked. "It's bad enough you almost broke my nose," he groaned. "Don't leave footprints on my sweatshirt."

Hammy pushed Zach's foot away and sat up on the floor. I could see that his nose was bleeding from being hit by the door.

"You're lucky Tyler didn't get a chance to hit you with his flashlight, you dork," Zach told him. "What are you doing here, anyway? "

"A.J. made a deal with me," Hammy told us. "He said he'd give me fifty bucks if I'd scare you guys out of the house. He figured that fifty bucks is a lot cheaper than two hundred."

"So you went along," I said.

"Sure," Hammy replied. "I could use the money. And besides, it would make a really funny story to tell the kids at school—how I scared you out of the house with a chain and a little evil laugh."

"What a jerk you are," Zach shouted as our friend stood up. "You'd sell out your best buddies for fifty bucks?"

"It's all a joke," Hammy replied. "Don't get your knickers in a knot."

I shook my head. That was my dad's phrase, "Don't get your knickers in a knot." It's an old phrase that means, "Don't blow your cool."

"So, why the chain?" I asked him.

"What did you expect me to do?" Hammy asked. "I mean, if I started going, "Whoooo,

whoooo," like a ghost, you'd know it was me by my voice. Besides, I remembered the chain thing from that movie, you know, *Night of the Living Zombies*. Were you scared, Tyler?"

"No, not me," I lied. "We figured you were some homeless guy, that's all. Just some guy that crashed for the night."

"Hammy," my brother announced, "you've got to pay for this. There's no way we're going to let you off easy after you tried to sell us out. You are guilty of selling out your friends."

"Okay," Hammy grunted. "I fall on the mercy of the court, or whatever you say."

"So, here's the deal. You have to stay here all night with us or we tell everybody that you're a rat."

"I can't stay all night. My mom will kill me," Hammy whined. "Worse, she'll call the police and tell them that I'm missing."

"Okay," I said to keep the two of them from getting into a fight. "You hang around until midnight, and then we let you go. A rat has to pay for being a rat." I looked down at my watch to see what time it was, but my watch had stopped at five o'clock when we climbed into the house.

"Yeah, you can join us in being bored to death," Zach told him. "The batteries on my MP3 player are dead, and Tyler's flashlight is half-dead. We're going to spend the night deaf and blind."

"Too bad," Hammy said. "There's a bunch of old newspapers in that first room I went in. Maybe if we took them down to the window at the end of the hall, we'd have enough light to look at them."

What a strange house, I thought to myself. There were bits and pieces of furniture, dust balls, and rotten plaster—all that made sense. But now a room filled with newspapers?

The three of us walked back to the first bedroom at the top of the stairs. The door was already open from when Hammy had smashed it with the chain. Inside, just as he said, were piles of yellowed newspapers.

"It looks like a collection," my brother said, a little surprised.

He was right. The papers weren't scattered over the floor; they were neatly stacked. The rest of the house was a mess, but this room looked like it had been kept pretty clean and neat.

"I wonder how old they are," I said, stepping into the dark room. "If this dumb flashlight would just work a little better…"

I pushed the switch one more time, and suddenly we had light. The flashlight cast a bright beam over the stacks of newspapers.

"I thought you said the battery was dead," my brother said.

"I told you that the storm was doing something funny," I replied. "Try your MP3 player."

Zach did as I asked, and suddenly there was a smile on his face. "Hey, I've got tunes!"

And I've got something I'm supposed to read, I said to myself. There was something funny going on in this place, something that I couldn't quite explain. But there seemed to be a clue right in front of us.

The newspaper at the top of the first pile had a large headline that glowed under the light from my flashlight: BLACKWOOD MURDER VERDICT!

CHAPTER 6

Let me admit, right now, that all of us like murder stories. I guess there are other guys who like sci-fi, or animal stories, or even romance. But not us. We've always been hooked on blood and gore. If a bunch of people get shot in a bank robbery, we want to read about it. Even worse, we want to see pictures.

Teachers don't like that much. In school, we're supposed to read history novels. You'd think there'd be lots of blood and gore in history, but not in the stuff they make us read. So Hammy brings in the books we like, the kind where a psycho chops up half the kids in a high school. That's our real reading. If only we could do book reports on them, our marks would be a lot better.

So you can see why the headline was a real grabber. Maybe someone was murdered in this old house.

Instead of us all trying to read the same paper, we got my brother to read out loud.

"August 16, 1964," Zach began. "Jurors reached a verdict today in the Blackwood murder case. Andrew Blackwood was found guilty of the murder of his brother, Charles Blackwood."

"He murdered his own brother!" Zach said, looking up. "That's wild!"

"Well, there are times I'd like to kill you, too," I joked. "But the thought of all that blood is too disgusting."

"Would you guys just keep quiet? Zach, keep reading!" Hammy said.

My brother read on. "The case has been in the national news because of the prominent Blackwood family. What does *prominent* mean?"

"It's like rich and famous," Hammy told him.

"The bloody killing came as a shock to the local

townspeople. A second shock came when charges were filed against 17-year-old Andrew Blackwood. Andrew Blackwood is the second son of the local lumber baron, Algernon Blackwood."

"What's a lumber baron?" Zach asked.

"It means the old man made a ton of money in the lumber business."

"Listen to this," Zach went on. "Charles Blackwood was stabbed sixteen times. The murder weapon was later found to be a knife from the Blackwood's own kitchen."

"Gross," I said.

My brother kept on reading, with all the details. The paper had interviews with the lawyers, the neighbors, even kids who went to private school with the two Blackwood brothers. No one could make sense of the murder. They were both "nice boys," according to one headline.

"Yeah, real nice," I said.

"But look here," Hammy said, pointing at the news story. "Guess when the murder happened?"

Zach looked to where Hammy's finger pointed. The date was October 29, 1963. "That's…" His

voice dropped off.

"Today. Today is October twenty-ninth," I said, finishing up for him.

"Creepy," Hammy said, and I think all three of us felt a little jab of fear. "Let's see what time it happened."

Now all three of us were pushing to look at the paper. Zach found it first. "The time of death was estimated at eleven o'clock," he read.

"What time is it now?" Hammy asked. "It must be almost eleven."

None of us really knew. My watch had stopped during the storm, so there was no way of telling how late it was.

"So, what's your point?" I asked him.

"It's just that the murder happened so many years ago tonight... soon. This is kind of the anniversary."

"Sick anniversary, if you ask me," I shot back.

"Well, this whole thing is pretty strange," Zach said. I think we were all feeling the same thing.

My brother grabbed a couple more papers from the pile. "Look at this stack of papers. Each one of them has a story about the murder."

"Pretty sick," I said. "Maybe their dad kept all these."

"But look here," Hammy said, picking up another paper. "This one has pictures of the two Blackwood kids."

"Yeah, so?" I said, beaming the flashlight at the pictures.

"I hate to say it," Hammy whispered as the three of us looked down, "but those two Blackwood brothers look just like... like you guys."

CHAPTER 7

"I look better than that guy," Zach snapped back. "I mean, I've got cool hair, not that geek grease look."

"Me, too," I said. "I'm way cooler than those guys."

That's what we said, but both of us were covering up what we felt. The Blackwood boys had long hair, like most kids had back in the 1960s, and they both had a funny, blank look in their eyes. But otherwise, they looked just like us.

"Hey, Zach," I laughed, "do me a favor and don't kill me, okay?"

"Well, I don't know. Sometimes you're a jerk,

Tyler, but I guess you're the best brother I have."

"Yeah, and sometimes I like you, too."

"Excuse me while I go off and puke," Hammy broke in. "You guys make fun of all this, but you've got to admit that something strange is going on. I mean, the two of you are here in the Blackwood house—on this particular night. Don't tell me it doesn't mean anything."

"It doesn't mean anything," I said, trying to get a laugh. "There are no such things as ghosts or people coming back in someone else's body. That's just in the movies."

I was the oldest guy, the one who had to stay reasonable. But even as the words came out, I felt scared. Hammy was right. There were too many strange things going on. The house, the flashlight, the newspapers, the pictures. It was all pointing one way, and I didn't like the way it was pointing.

"Okay, I've got an idea," I told the other two. I tried to stay cool, to sound as if I wasn't scared or upset. "Let's call off this stupid bet and get out of here. A.J. cheated by sending Hammy to scare us, so I say, enough is enough. We've stayed here long enough. Hammy is a witness. It's cold and wet, and there are mice. So I say we call the whole thing off and go home."

"I've got an even better idea," Zach said. "I say we prorate the bet."

Hammy and I both stared at him. "What's that supposed to mean?" I asked him.

"It means we stayed at least six hours out of twelve, or one-half. So we prorate and A.J. owes us one-half of two hundred bucks. That's a hundred bucks on the nose."

Have I mentioned that my brother is a math whiz?

It didn't take us long to make up our minds. Nobody wanted to admit being scared, of course. We talked about all the other stuff, instead. How stupid the whole bet was. How cold and damp and leaky the house was. How A.J. should get beaten up for sending Hammy to scare us.

Once we decided, it took us no time to pack up our stuff and head back down the stairs. I was waiting for my flashlight to go out, but it didn't. We had enough light to get down the stairs, and plenty of light to make our way to the window we had come in.

"So, where's the crowbar?" I asked Hammy.

"I don't know," he replied. "A.J. let me inside, and then he threw the crowbar onto the floor. It should be right here."

I shifted the beam of the flashlight all around the window, down to the floor, and then all around the room. No crowbar. Nothing that we could use to pry open the plywood.

"Okay, I'm going to kick it," I told them. That's what the guys on TV always do. They get stuck somewhere and just kick the door open—or the window, in this case.

So I gave the plywood a huge karate whack! It didn't move.

"Did A.J. nail us in here, or what?" I shouted. "This stuff isn't stuck on with just duct tape."

"There were a couple of nails at the top when I came in, but it was easy to pull it back," Hammy said. "Let me just..." Then he tried to push the plywood out so we could get through. In a second,

Zach and I were pushing with him. Still, the plywood didn't move.

"We're trapped," Zach said, and then added a few swear words to go with it.

This time I didn't tell him to watch his mouth. Instead, I grabbed a hunk of baseboard that was lying on the floor. I took the board and aimed a big whack at the plywood.

CRA-ACK!

The plywood made so much noise, you'd think it would break in half. But it didn't move.

KA-BOOM! A peal of thunder came from over our heads. And then the flashlight went out.

There we were, the three of us, stuck in total darkness. We were trapped in the Blackwood house just as the storm roared back to life. And, I swear, I heard some kind of sound deep in the house.

"I don't like this," I whispered to the others.

CHAPTER 8

The three of us stood in the darkened room, staring at the plywood on the window. Hammy was shaking his head, I was feeling a little creepy, and my brother was mad.

"If A.J. nailed that plywood back on, I'm going to kill him," Zach said.

"Not a good idea," Hammy said. "Look what happened to the guy in the paper."

"Yeah, right," Zach agreed. "So I'll just give him terrible pain and suffering. Maybe I'll tell Tasha Lebinski that he's got the hots for her."

The two of them laughed. I had to admire them. Zach and Hammy still seemed pretty cool, despite what had gone on. Me, I was scared. I tried hard to hide it from the other guys, but inside I was shaking. Too much of this was just too weird. And now we were stuck in the Blackwood house for the whole night.

"I've got an idea," my brother said. "It sounds like a lot of branches are blowing up against the house. Maybe we can get out through one of the upstairs windows and then climb down a tree."

I had to hand it to Zach—that was the best idea anybody had come up with all night. All we had to do was get back up the stairs, including the busted one, in total darkness. The rest should be easy.

It took us almost no time to get up the staircase. Every so often there was a flash of lightning, so we could see our way. Zach got to the top first, followed by Hammy, followed by me. Nobody said much. All we could think about was getting out of the house.

Upstairs, there was a little more light, but the storm was back in full force. Thunder rattled the doors and windows. Lightning flashed across the night sky. The wind outside was like a hurricane.

"With a storm like this," Zach said, "I bet the lights are out all over town."

We couldn't see anything outside the windows. Even the moon was hidden behind the black storm clouds. Everything was dark, inside and out, except for the flashes of lightning.

"Let's try that window at the end of the hall," Zach said.

There was a large oak tree right outside the hall window. All we needed to do was open the window and get one good branch to hold on to.

"Push on your side," Zach told Hammy.

Zach pushed up on the right side, Hammy on the left . And the window didn't budge.

"Must be painted shut," Hammy told him.

"I bet nobody has tried to open a window here for thirty years," Zach said.

I didn't say anything. Some part of me knew that the window wouldn't open. Some part of me knew that none of the windows would open for us. I knew, somehow, that the three of us were trapped here for a reason. But I didn't know what the reason could be.

Zach and Hammy went off into a bedroom to try another window. I followed behind them, even though I knew it was useless. I didn't know what was going to happen to us, but there was one thing I knew for sure—I didn't want to be alone. I was scared, and I didn't want to face it alone.

"This is stupid!" Zach shouted. "None of these windows is going to open." A sudden flash of lightning let me see his face. It was covered with sweat and dirt.

"We could smash one," Hammy suggested.

KA-BOOM! The thunder came crashing down like a deafening answer.

"I guess," Zach replied. "Somebody might hear and call the cops, but at least we'd be out of here."

He had just finished talking when the first sound came: *BONG!*

"What the..." Hammy began. A second later, the sound came again, from somewhere deep in the house.

BONG!

"It's a bell," I told them. "It sounds like the chime of a big old clock."

BONG!

"But how could there be a working clock in this old place?" Zach asked. "And how come we didn't hear it before?"

BONG!

"I don't know about you guys," Hammy said, "but I say we break a window and get out of here."

BONG!

My brother agreed. Quickly, Zach picked up a hunk of two-by-four from the floor and smashed it against the window glass.

BONG!

The glass didn't break.

"Here, let me try it," Hammy said. He took the piece of wood and, again, smashed it into the glass.

BONG!

The glass might as well have been steel. "Here, Tyler, you try it!" Hammy shouted as he handed the wood to me.

BONG!

I was the strongest guy, but I knew it was useless. I swung the wood against the glass once,

twice, three times.

BONG!

The glass didn't even move. Zach grabbed the wood from me and threw it at the window with all his strength.

BONG!

There was lightning outside. We could see that the glass hadn't even cracked. "This is so stupid!" Zach cried, his face flashing anger in the flash of light.

BONG! Went the chime. *KA-BOOM!* Roared the thunder.

Then it was quiet. The storm suddenly died down, and the bell stopped ringing. The only sound we could hear was the three of us breathing heavily.

"Eleven o'clock," I said. I had been counting the bells. "It's that time—the time of the murder."

"And we're trapped," Hammy sighed.

Then my brother spoke up in a very high, very scared voice. "I don't like this. I don't like this at all."

CHAPTER 9

"Okay, let's be sensible," Hammy said. I knew he was scared. I could tell by his voice and the strange way he talked.

"Yeah, right," my brother replied. He was trying to get his head straight, trying to make something real out of what was happening to us.

"We're in some kind of trouble," Hammy went on. "So, what do you do when you're in trouble?"

"Call the cops," I said.

"Did anybody bring a cell phone?" Hammy asked.

The silence told the story. It would have been too sensible to bring a cell phone. It would have been too sensible to bring an extra flashlight, or a crowbar, or even matches. We hadn't come prepared. We thought a night in this old house would be a joke, a laugh, a walk in the park.

"So, what have we got?" Hammy went on.

He was trying hard. Everything around us was crazy. Everything around us was weird. But Hammy was trying to bring us back to real life.

"A busted flashlight, a couple of books, sleeping bags, my MP3 player, us," Zach said.

"And what's our problem?"

"We can't get out of this place," I said, making it dead simple.

"How come?" he asked.

"The ghosts won't let us," I whispered.

The two of them turned and stared at me. I could see my brother in the faint light from outside. He was shaking. I knew that Hammy was scared, too, but he just looked angry.

"Wrong!" Zach shouted. "Tyler, you've got to snap out of it! There's some strange stuff going on, but there's no such thing as ghosts."

"Right," Hammy agreed. "We've got windows

that won't open and won't break, so maybe it's real tough glass. Maybe in the old days the glass was thicker."

"Maybe it's tempered glass, like the stuff in car windows," Zach suggested.

"Sure, I bet that's it," Hammy agreed. "Old man Blackwood was real rich, and he could buy the best of everything. He probably got windows made out of tempered glass."

"So our best bet is to go back downstairs and pry open that piece of plywood," Hammy said. "If we still had the crowbar..."

"They took it," I muttered. Some part of me knew that the ghosts had taken it, to trap us here.

Hammy and Zach just ignored me.

"Maybe we can get a piece of metal off that old bed," Zach told Hammy. "Maybe we could wedge that into the plywood and use it like a crowbar."

"Now you're thinking," Hammy said, and even his voice was smiling.

The two of them took off to the bedroom where Zach and I had hidden earlier. In seconds they were pulling at the metal bed frame. The two of them made so much noise it would have been enough to wake the dead. Sadly, I was very sure that the dead were already awake—and that they were watching us.

"Twist it," Hammy shouted. He and Zach were trying to free up one of the bars that held the bedsprings to the frame. The two of them working together did the job. Zach proudly held a piece of metal over his head.

"Hey, even if we can't get out, at least we have a weapon," he said. "Come on, ghosts, we're ready for you now!"

"Shhhh!" I said.

"Tyler, you've really lost it. I can't believe my older brother has turned out to be such a wimp."

I said nothing more. I knew a hunk of steel wouldn't stop the ghosts who were after us. I knew that nothing would get us out of this house until this night—this anniversary—was over. Maybe, maybe then, they'd let us go. Or maybe we'd be dead, ourselves.

The three of us went back downstairs, a little faster than before. I think Zach and Hammy both felt better with that piece of metal in their hands.

It only took a minute to get down to the window where we had come in. I still held the flashlight as we came into the room, and suddenly the light came back on.

All three of us stopped cold at what we saw.

"The crowbar!" Hammy cried out.

"I swear it wasn't down here before," I told them. "We all looked."

But the crowbar was right in front of us now, right in front of the window, right where we would have stepped on it earlier.

"Somebody's playing games with us," Zach cried out. Then he began shouting at the top of his lungs, "HEY, WE KNOW WHAT YOU'RE DOING. DON'T THINK YOU CAN SCARE US."

He handed the piece of metal to Hammy, and then took the crowbar in his own hands.

"I've had enough of this sick joke," he muttered. He took the crowbar and jammed it between the window frame and the plywood. Then he began to pull.

"It's moving!" he cried out. "Tyler, help me pull on this."

The two of us both grabbed the crowbar and pulled with all our might. We could hear a creak from the plywood and feel a small movement, but then the crowbar lost its wedge. The two of us went flying backward.

Seconds later, Zach and I were lying on the floor. I must have knocked myself on something, because I could taste blood in my mouth.

"You've got to get the crowbar stuck in there," Hammy told us, as if we didn't know. He picked up the crowbar, wedged it between the plywood and the frame, and then hit it with the piece of metal from the bed frame.

"Like that," he announced.

This time, Hammy and Zach tried to pry the plywood. I aimed the flashlight at the window and could see the plywood move.

"We've almost got it!" my brother cried out.

And they almost *did* have one corner free. They had almost enough space to get the smallest guy out.

But suddenly the three of us knew there was somebody else in the room with us.

I'm not sure how we all knew the same thing at once. It wasn't as if there was a big sound, or the chiming of a bell, or a moan. There was no sound at all; just the hiss of rain outside the house. But we all knew that we weren't alone.

Zach and Hammy stopped working at the plywood. Hammy grabbed at the piece of metal and held it like a gun. Zach took the crowbar with both hands. All three of us turned and looked back into the darkness of the house.

"WE HEAR YOU!" Zach shouted, his voice high and shrieking.

"Shine the light on it!" Hammy ordered.

The word *it* kept going through my brain. Now they knew what I had known before. We were not dealing with a joke from A.J., or some homeless guy, or anything from this world. We were dealing with ghosts, real ghosts.

I raised the flashlight and pointed the beam of light around the room, across the hall, and then back at the stairs.

"Oh my gawd!" Zach cried out.

CHAPTER 10

There is a place you can get to that is beyond fear. There is a place in your soul that is so scared, so hopeless, that you can't feel fear anymore. There is a place that is so full of despair that you just go numb.

I had reached that place.

In front of us was a shape, the shape of a man, but it was not a living man. We could half see through the shape, which was like a tower of dust or a plume of smoke. But the shape was neither dust nor smoke—it had a head, arms, legs, and a body. It was something real, but not something from this world.

Somehow, I knew this had to happen. Even as the shape moved in front of the stairs, I was not surprised. I'd been waiting for it—for him—ever since we had come to this house. Some part of me knew that we were small players in a big drama, and that we had some part to play on this night. The anniversary.

While the others stood frozen, I somehow found my voice. "What do you want?" I called out.

There was no sound. Even the storm outside had fallen silent. The wind had dropped off, and the trees were still.

In the silence, the shape moved. An arm—or what should have been an arm—lifted from its body. A hand appeared at the end of that arm, a hand that was just bone and smoke. The whole shape turned slightly, and the arm, the hand, and the single bone of a finger pointed.

It pointed at my brother.

"We've got to get out of here," Hammy said in a whisper. He was the only one with any sense left. My brother and I were frozen, powerless.

"Let's roll!" Hammy cried.

I felt that I couldn't move. My feet, my legs, my whole body was frozen. I wanted to run, to scream, to hide. I wanted to strike out and protect Zach from this THING! This thing and what it wanted. I so wanted to move, but I was frozen in my own body.

"Move!" Hammy cried.

Then he grabbed me, tugging on my sweatshirt until I was moving. He kept pulling me away from the thing, and somehow I began to walk. My feet seemed to weigh a thousand pounds, but thanks to Hammy they took steps, they walked, and then they ran.

"Faster," I heard Zach shout.

In seconds we had escaped from the living room and were racing down the hall. Hammy pushed at a door and suddenly we were in another room, a ballroom or a library. I ran my flashlight beam over the walls and saw empty shelves with a handful of books still on them. Just to the right was a big, old bookcase, like you see in antique stores. It was made of oak and was bigger than both Hammy and me.

"Push the bookcase in front of the door," Hammy ordered.

I could hear his heavy breathing as he got beside the bookcase and began to push. Hammy must have found some strength from somewhere. Or maybe it came from me.

I felt so weak. It seemed as if my hands and feet were so heavy that I couldn't even lift them. The bookcase was too big, and I was too weak. And so tired. Still, I joined with Hammy and pushed with

him. Slowly the old bookcase began to move. Maybe we could have gotten it in front of the door, but we had a bigger problem.

"Wait a minute! Where's Zach?" Hammy asked.

"He was…" I began, and then the words fell to nothing. I thought he was right behind us. I thought I had heard him running behind me as we went down the hall. I thought I had heard him pull around the door and come into the library with us.

"Zach!" Hammy screamed.

Again, silence was our only answer.

"Give me the light," Hammy said. He took the flashlight from my numb hands and sent the beam all over the room. Then he swore.

"Stay here," he told me. "I'm going to get him."

In a second he was out the door, and I heard his footsteps running down the hall. He had the flashlight, so the library was dark as coal.

Then Hammy's footsteps stopped. There was no cry, no grunt, no shout of surprise. There was only silence throughout the entire house.

And I was alone.

Chapter 11

Some moments in your life you can never forget. Those moments can take no time at all—a second, or even a fraction of a second—but in your mind they can last forever. They get played and replayed, over and over, from all the angles. They come back, even if you tell yourself that you're done with them. Even if you say you're bored with them. Even if it's useless to think about them.

I'll tell you about the first moment like that. It was the day my dad died, the moment in our living room when the man from the logging company stood with my mother and told us. That was one moment. I still keep playing that over, changing it.

I make him say that dad was hurt, but he'll be okay. Sometimes I make him say that we won the lottery and got a ton of money. But mostly I just see his face, and mom's face, and feel the beating in my heart.

Now I'd had another awful moment—the shape, the ghost, pointing at Zach. I couldn't get that moment out of my mind. I kept thinking of what I should have done. I should have charged at the thing. I should have smashed the stupid bones with my fists. I'd never let a real person hurt my brother, never. But I had just stood there while the thing pointed at him, marking him. Now the thing had taken Zach. I could feel it. I could hear Zach's screams inside my head, even if there was no sound in the house.

And I was alone. My arms and legs felt heavy. My hands were tight and frozen. There was no sound in the house. I could hear some water dripping from the storm. But there was no other sound. Nothing from my brother. Nothing from Hammy.

What do I do now? I asked myself. *What am I*

supposed to do now?

Maybe they were the same question. Maybe I was trapped by what was going to happen. Maybe my life was trapped by fate, just as my body was trapped in the house.

Then I heard steps out in the hallway. "Hammy!" I shouted. "Zach!" I cried. There was no answer, but the steps were human steps, not the footfalls of a ghost.

Then I froze. I'd called out. I'd let the ghosts hear where I was. I wasn't hiding anymore. I was just waiting for them to come. I was just waiting for them to take me, the way they'd taken my kid brother.

Think, I told myself. If I could just make some sense of all this. If I could just figure out what they wanted. Maybe. Maybe what? Maybe I could stop them. Maybe I could end this and rescue my brother. Maybe I could break the curse that trapped us all in this bizarre old house.

It's an anniversary, I said to myself. What do people do on an anniversary? They think back about old times. But these ghosts weren't people.

What would they think back about? A murder? What would they do? And why would they want my brother?

I stepped outside the library and looked down the silent hall. The house was pitch black. I couldn't even see a glow from the flashlight I'd given Hammy.

They've got him, too, I said to myself. *Now it's just me. I'm the last one.*

I could go back into the library and try to hide, but they knew where I was. I could go back to the living room and try to push my way out the window. But the ghosts might be there, waiting.

Or I could face them.

Face them, I said to myself, almost as if some other voice was coming into my head.

Slowly I walked back into the living room. It was so dark, I had to feel my way down the hall. One step at a time, back, back.

Then my foot touched something. I could hear the ring of metal as I kicked it. I bent over to touch with my fingers what I'd hit with my foot. I groped on the floor, blind in the darkness, and then, at last,

I had it.

A knife, I said to myself.

I picked it up carefully and clutched the handle. It was a good-sized knife, pointed and sharp. But it didn't feel like a hunting knife. It felt like the kind of knife my mom might use in the kitchen.

A kitchen knife, I repeated to myself, *just like the knife used in the murder.*

I screamed. My scream was a wild, inhuman cry. It was the scream of a guy who was trapped in the worst way. Suddenly I knew what they wanted, and I knew what had to happen.

"NO!" I shouted at the top of my lungs.

I threw the knife away. It went bouncing along the floor until it came to a stop halfway into the living room.

"I WON'T BE PART OF IT!" I screamed out to them. "I WON'T ACT OUT YOUR ANNIVERSARY!" I started cursing, swearing at the top of my lungs. When it was over, when the last of my strength was gone, I sat down on the floor.

And I started to cry.

It was the lowest moment of my life. I wasn't a

teenager anymore. I was a blind, crying, helpless boy. I had never before felt so terribly alone, so terribly afraid.

"Dad!" I cried out, for no reason that made any sense. I wanted my dad to come back, to be with me. If I was going to die on this floor, in this house, I just wanted my dad. Was that too much to ask?

There was no answer to my cry. There was no sudden miracle to get me off the floor and out of the house. I sat there, sobbing, waiting to die.

Then I heard the footsteps. From somewhere, deeper in the house, there were footsteps that I knew. And then a voice.

"Where are you?" the voice called out.

It was my brother, Zach, alive! And he was looking for me.

"Hey, Tyler, where are you?" he asked. There was an echo to his voice, as if he were way down in a long tunnel.

"I'm here," I said, wiping away the tears. I had to stop sobbing. I had to stop being such a loser.

I heard Zach coming toward me. His steps were slow and careful in the darkened house.

I stood up. I'm not sure why I stood up, but something deep inside me said that I needed to. Something inside me was telling me to get ready—that the worst was still to come.

I heard his breathing now, as my brother came toward me. Then there was the clunk of metal, and Zach stopped. I heard a strange cry come from him, a terrible cry. He sounded like an animal caught in a trap, begging for life, or begging to die.

"I don't want to do this," Zach panted.

And then I knew he had picked up the knife. I knew he had the knife in his hand, and he was coming toward me.

"Fight them!" I cried.

"They're too strong," he said, his voice struggling against the words. "I don't want to do this, Charlie, but the voices…"

I could see a glint of light from the knife as he came toward me.

"I'm not Charlie!" I screamed. "You're not Andrew! Put the knife down!"

But Zach didn't put the knife down. He kept coming at me, forcing me against the wall. I had no

strength to fight, no strength even to put up my arms against him. I just stood there, waiting for the end.

"Dad," I cried out as Zach raised the knife over his head, "stop him!"

CHAPTER 12

The sun coming through the window woke me up. I blinked a couple of times, wondering where I was. Then it all came back—the Blackwood house, the bet with A.J., the nightmare.

I looked over at the other sleeping bag, and there was my brother, Zach. He was covered in blood.

"Zach, wake up," I said, reaching over to shake him.

My brother opened his eyes and looked at me. He sat up on one arm and coughed a few times. "I just had this awful dream," he said. Then his voice dropped, as if the dream were too awful to talk about. "Sheesh, look at this blood," he said. "I must have had a nosebleed last night."

I looked down at myself, wondering if there was blood on me, too. But there was nothing on my clothes that I could see. I was just the way I had been last night, except a little stiff from sleeping on the floor. And I felt a strange pain in my chest.

"Hey, did we win the bet yet?" Zach asked.

I looked at my watch, but it was still stopped at the time of the storm. "Can't tell for sure," I told him. "It looks like morning outside, so I declare us the winners. Let's get out of this place before the mice wake up."

We rolled up our sleeping bags and put on our backpacks. The night was over, and the new day was shining brightly outside.

"I had this weird dream," Zach muttered. "There were ghosts, and Hammy, and a knife."

"Funny, but I think I had the same dream," I told him. "In my dream, you tried to stab me, just like the brother in the newspaper articles."

"Yeah, my dream had the newspaper part, but I don't remember stabbing you," Zach said.

"I guess you didn't get the whole dream, just the cut-down version," I told him.

"So, did I kill you, or what?" he asked.

"Guess not," I told him. "I'm still here. And as far as I can see, I'm in pretty good shape."

"Yeah, well, you don't see all that well," Zach said, staring at me. "You've got a big red spot on your sweatshirt that looks like blood."

He wasn't kidding. I looked down at my sweatshirt and saw a perfect circle of blood. Suddenly I could feel my heart beating inside me. It all came back—the fear, the knife, the pain of the blade as it sliced into me.

I lifted my sweatshirt and tried to look at my chest, but I couldn't see much without a mirror. *This is weird*, I thought, *but a dream is only a dream.*

Of course, Zach didn't need a mirror. "Look at that, Tyler," he cried. "You've got some kind of a scar right in the middle of your chest. It's like somebody stabbed you with a knife!"

I was going to say something, when we both heard a noise outside.

Down below, on the lawn, were Hammy and A.J. Hammy was grinning from ear to ear. And A.J. was shouting, "Get up, you jerks, you won the bet." ■

Published in the United States of America by:

꘎ Dominie Press, Inc.
1949 Kellogg Avenue
Carlsbad, California 92008 USA

www.dominie.com

ISBN 0-7685-2357-5
Printed in Singapore by PH Productions Pte Ltd
1 2 3 4 5 PH 08 07 06 05 04